The Mountain

Contents

Mountain 13
Draugr 14
Reckoning 14
Soon 15
Foresight 16
Flood 16
Eventide 17
Kenning 17
Bayside 18
Fortune 18
Black-out 19
Narcissus 20
Light 20
Spiral 21
Circle 21
Ascend 21
Sun-shadow 22
Night garden 22
Perspective 22
Shine 22
Journey 23
To the ends of the earth 23
Unease 24
A sacrifice 24

The Mountain

Ravens 24
Hidden 25
Sensate 25
The tree 26
Ghost-hunt 26
Prayerless 27
North and south 28
Gust 29
Adelaide Street 29
Pattern 29
Day six 29
December 30
Haunted 30
R.I.P. Daisy (16/11/2017) 30
Year long 32
Sickness 32
Woman asleep on train 33
Father 33
Wednesday 34
Mirror 34
Stendec 34
Smart phone 35
Parley 35
Sisu 35
Thursday the 19th 36

The Mountain

L'enfer c'est les autres 37
20 years 37
Aeons 37
Monday 38
Unbalanced 38
Mirror 39
Sunder 39
Call 39
Love 40
Fallen 40
Geasa 40
Muse 41
Grace 42
Cliffs above the bay 42
We all remember our first 42
The signs 44
Alchemy 44
Stasis 45
Perth 45
Gate 46
Hourglass 46
Firmament 46
Migraines, deserts 47
The test 47
Stockholm 48

The Mountain

40th 48
Sickness 49
June 49
Training 49
Nemo iudex in causa sua 50
No harvest 50
Team function 50
Pebble 51
Forge 51
Clouded skies 52
Better left unsaid 52
33 1/3 52
Prosopagnosia 53
Fading of the day 53
Hero 54
Tuath Dé 54
Cuchulainn 55
Beneath Yggdrasil's boughs 55
Obituary 56
Water's edge 57
High tide, low 57
Black, and white 58
25 April 58
Icarus 59
Working late 60

The Mountain

Shadow 60
Flood 61
Literary contortionism 61
Effort 62
Eight directions 62
Circles 62
Elysia 63
Winter skies in Autumn 63
By these signs 63
Forgive 64
Next 64
Camden Haven 64
Change 65
Half 65
Question 66
Mirrors 66
Anodyne seas 66
Oil and water 67
Tree fall 67
Moment(um) 68
The first stone 68
The night before 69
All, and nothing 69
Fool 69
Facebook 70

The Mountain

Knowing, unknowing 70
Unnamed 70
Vanity Fair 71
Annus 72
Birdsong 72
Red cloud 72
Crowd, silence 73
Remains of the hours 73
Sun, and air 73
Leaf 74
Through gates 74
Walls 75
Chrysalis 75
The surface and the water deep 76
One 77
Anatomy 78
Binary 78
What remains 79
Absolute 79
Overreach 80
Waking 80
Poetry? 81
A few words 81
Wasted effort 82
Unknowing 82

The Mountain

Mirror 82
Leaves 83
Madding crowd 83
Causa mortis 84
Fever 84
Useful Idiot 84
Ephemeral 85
The bay of every 85
The sound of 86
Frame 86
Perception 87
Peregrinus mens 87
City office 88
Thoughts 88
Sol 89
Going home 89
In quiet places 89
Et tu? 90
Simplicity 90
Obol 91
Unwritten 91
Sun-warmed shoulders and countless skies 91
Leaves in the wind 91
Shadows fall 92
Zero sum 92

The Mountain

And thus, I perceived it 92
Neither 93
Unfallen (RIP Tony Rokov) 93
Until next time 93
Words 94
Sisyphus 94
Under which we march 94
Within 95
Distill 95
Write a poem 95
All 95
Brick walls 96
Uncertainty 96
Turn to home 97
Change 97
Bury 97
Rise and fall 98
Highway 98
War 98
Shine 99
Dam walls 99
Memoria in aeterna 99
Au courant 99
Fire 100
Absolute 100

The Mountain

Hidden in plain view 100
Aeon 100
Form 100
Importance 101
Extremes 101
Tide 101
Tea 101
Waves 102
September 102
Morning star 102
Mirage 102
Storm's end 102
Mountain road 103
Enervation 103
Wolf 103
Five rivers 103
The bow, the sunlit glade 104
Steel 104
Poet 104
Momentum 105
Anxiety 105
Atonement 105
Automation 105
Tools 106
Crossroads 106

The Mountain

Lost words	106
Paths well worn	107
Jewel	107
Complete	107
Roster's end	107
Beloved	108
A narrow path	108
Perhaps	108
Locus	109
Eating lunch	109
A new day	110
Artificial	110
Change	110
Why the silence	110
Tidings	111
Again	111
Morning	111
Mania	111
Sunlight	112
Sol	112
Quietude	112
Impermanence	112
Paradigm	112
Pilbara	113
Illusion, delusion	113

The Mountain

The passing of a man (a belated eulogy) 113
Beyond the fences 114
Sunday 115
Hurt, wrong and anger 115
Different 115
Waste 115
Waters 116
Not forgotten, unknown 116
Blood 116
Empty vessels 116
Perception 117
Turning 117
Withdrawal symptoms 117
Mercy 117
Old fashioned 118
Breath 118
Brevity 118
Moment 118
Fight through 118
Eyes cast down 119
Offering 119
Names, labels 119
Winding 119
Paresthesia 120
Blade 120

The Mountain

Sparks 121
Drain 121
Dragonflies 121
Conference 121
Wanderer 122
I? 122
Dream 123
Haven 123
Part 123

Mountain

I
am the
mountain

Under searing suns
the mountain shades

Through doubtful fogs
the mountain rises

Midst tempest and storm
the mountain stands

In harrow and war
the mountain unmoved

Beneath darkening skies
the mountain shelters

Over hubbub and clamour
the mountain still

Among tumult and tide
the mountain alone, unlonely

Between heaven and earth
the mountain is

I
am the

The Mountain

mountain

Draugr

I saw him
again
dead, not dead
alive, unliving
unaware of both
lightless eye
soulless breath
his shadow
more alive
than he

O father
having slain you once
must I
cut you down again
or is this
not you, but another
wearing your face?

It matters not

Done
what is needed
to be done

Reckoning

I slew and deep

The Mountain

I buried them
thinking I was free

They stand
and watch
in silence

Always beyond
reach, beyond
my rage, tears, curses

They stand
and watch
in silence

Death's bed, I lie
as shadows fall
paler than my sins

They stand
and wait
in silence

Soon

Soon
my heat will not beat
breath will cease
A ripple
in the current
of the stream
dissolved

Foresight

Why am I shown
what is to come
without hope of change
or of escape?

Knowing the wound to come
(a wounding in itself)
a blessing, curse
both, or neither?

Foresight, a sentence
certainty of execution
without knowing when
only what, and how

All that can be done
is to wait, endure
face what is, will
come to pass

Flood

The currents quickening
waters rise
maelstrom maw
strange shores scoured

The Mountain

Eventide

On the edges
of shadow
in shadow
they live
Only by the sword
of mind, soul
shall they fear
and be slain
I watch
I sharpen
and I hone

Kenning

Between this world
and another
seeing, hearing, sensing
that which is
those who are
here, not there
there, not here

Who, and what
so different to you
neither good, nor evil
be named
they simply are

Between the waking

The Mountain

and sleep
thinner the veil
diaphanous, tenuous
as it already was

Yet I remain
here, and there
there, and here
neither one
the other
but both

Bayside

I walked the bay
over the headland
Brisbane summer
tropical ulcer heat
once mangroves, now mud
algae-diseased
Hel's breath-wind
sharp, fetid taste
like a slaughterhouse

Fortune

I stand atop
vanquished foes
many of whom
wore my face

The Mountain

One by one
or by many
they came
or were called out
one by one
or by many
they fell

Yet you, fool
declare my fortune
won by luck
gifted unto me
ignoring blood
scars
offerings, sacrifice
the notch-blade ax
at my side

Many foes can give
a man but one death
I stand atop
vanquished foes
and will stand
even when
I fall

Black-out

No light except
cloud-dimmed moon

The Mountain

no sound but for
rain-drummed roofs

Narcissus

Rose-scent
overpowers the room
some smiled
my teeth bared
I could smell
decay, rot beneath
not quite hidden
dragon-stench on gold
incense on the corpse
the glamour of the monster

Light

When realising
nothing
has colour
everything
a spectrum reflects
that even
in darkest shade
we are bathed
by light

Oh, how the world
Shines

Spiral

Solitude arising
from strength
strength arising
from solitude

Circle

In the beginning
was the ending
the wheel turns
above, below
within, without

Ascend

I ascend the peak
leaving flesh behind
seeking heaven
until the mind, stars
themselves fall away
what is, was, I
no more than a ripple
dissolved in the stream

Sun-shadow

We are all Sisyphus
she mused
reflections of Camus
of toil
its own reward
and worlds
within worlds

Night garden

The tree reached down
brushed my head
I stood
among the vines
stars burning cold

Perspective

The brighter the sun
the darker the shadows
The darker the shadows
the brighter the sun

Shine

In the dawn sunlight

The Mountain

      sudden breezes sweep
      diamond-dew from trees

      What pen or tongue
      could ever
      truly, fully
      describe heaven?

Journey

      The waves lap
      tide ascending
      looking beyond
      the sunlight
      firmament vast
      awaits me

To the ends of the earth

      South
      beyond road's end
      where no fires of man
      offer smoke to the skies
      no field nor furrow
      through lands cold, wild
      I walk ever on

Unease

Autumn winds tug
fleece at my collar
Hraesvelgr stirs

Ravens no longer
at my shoulder
no wolf at my heel

Minds and souls
of men rust, corrode
alongside their spears

A sacrifice

Irmin's Way is darkened
hidden by wandering clouds
waters cold cascade
over my upturned gaze

To unseen gods, unknown
I offer the ember's arc
the stone and the leaf
heart-flesh and toil

Ravens

As I walked among trees
ravens two spoke

thought and memory
calling me still
through the wood

Hidden

The gods are not gone
they remain
hidden and watchful
I see them without sight
hear them in silence profound
beseech them wordlessly

Where now are those
who would, could teach
their ways
rites and supplications

Masterless, unmastered
ignorant, I remain
hidden stay the gods
till time falls away
once more

Sensate

The prison of the senses
bound within
frequencies narrow
of physical perception

The Mountain

outside of which
we deludedly say
nothing else is

But what
if there
is more?

The tree

Roots descending
through three-fold realm
to beyonds
I ken not
the ash stands
eternal

I have the will
nine days and nights
hung, spear-pierced
offer myself
unto myself
sacrifice
but not yet
the knowledge or way

Ghost-hunt

The footsteps tread
across the room above

The Mountain

      yet I know
      the house
      is empty
      but for me

      Quietly I tread
      swiftly the stair
      but again
      empty halls I find
      solitude
      sunlit and shadowed

Prayerless

Do not look for banners
of relief on horizons
if they come, they come
if not, they do not
The gods will not
send you aid
they have already
gifted you
with will
breath and life

Trust only the spear
in your hand
shield on your arm
sinew forged of years

Laugh, and rejoice

The Mountain

> in the foe-press
> be victorious
> both in standing
> and falling
>
> The gods ask
> no more than this
> and no less

North and south

> This ancient land
> knows me not
> its secrets and spirits
> unrevealed
>
> I sense its gods
> hidden, watching
> the stranger, I
> the exile unwelcome
>
> My heart hearkens
> north, from where
> my kin dwelt and dwell
> lands and seas
>
> Manannán's wild heart
> Enbarr's flashing hooves
> the flight of Huginn and Muninn

Gust

Not out of nowhere
did the wind suddenly rise
laughter of the gods

Adelaide Street

The flowers held
like an ax
she strode as if to battle

Pattern

A few simple words
and the patterns become clear
a fog lifting from the valley

The wheel turns
without end
yet it only
touches the ground
once

Day six

I sat and watched
the mind

The Mountain

a phantasm spinning, contorting

The mirage convinced
of its own existence

December

Storm clouds overhead
swirling airs and raindrops
the city breathes in

Haunted

Ghosts of yesterday
unliving yet here
sustained
by my sorrow
regret, and guilt

I wander the halls
of my soul
and find them there
raging, or simply
staring back through me

R.I.P. Daisy (16/11/2017)

A knock on the door
sympathetic neighbour

The Mountain

and there she was
as if asleep
on the road
if the blood
were ignored

She was still warm
the breeze
ruffling her fur
but she was gone
it had been quick
a blow to the head
I moved her to safety
a simple cardboard box
removed her collar
for memory
washed the blood
from her nametag
off the road
and my hands

I dug her bed
in a quiet corner
of the garden
laid her down
arranged her limbs
as if she slumbered
in the warm sun
stroked her one last time
tears mixed with dirt

All this was easy
the dread, burden

The Mountain

question
of how to tell the kids
and when

Year long

It's been a long year
informative
and instructive
awakenings
stripping away
of delusions
expect now nothing
no one
stand, walk alone
yesterday never was
tomorrow will never be
give quarter, aid
but ask for
and seek none

Sickness

Circling fan
does little
but emphasise
the fever

The Mountain

Woman asleep on train

Blanketed by
mechanically cold air
and the introverted silence
of the carriage's crowd
she sits, eyes closed
her face calm
serene
head bowing
as if in silent prayer

She wakes
now and then
starting
a brief anxious look
before she slips again
beneath the peaceful waves

Father

The parallels
cannot be unseen
as much as I want
to deny them
face in the mirror
mannerisms
the not-quite-fitting-in
failed relationship, divorce
walking alone
too alike for comfort

The Mountain

my father's son
am I

Wednesday

Awoken
no thoughts other
than the wind
through leaves

Mirror

I polish
and polish
the mirror
sweep away dust
until it reflects
eternity
shines brighter
than the sun

Such foolishness
utter waste
there was never
a mirror at all

Stendec

I look like shit.

The Mountain

Well, more shit
than usual.
Problems self-posed
sans solution
corrode and erode

Smart phone

Eyes looking elsewhere
not here, anywhere but here
around us, heaven

Parley

My liege
I will bear thy missive

My brothers
guard well my arms
against my return
if I fall
I charge thee
quench well
their thirst

Sisu

Weariness
of the limbs

The Mountain

I know well
of the heart, soul
this is new
The road
cares not
will not
walk itself

Thursday the 19th

Something was wrong
I sensed it
growing as the train ground
towards the city
Central station crowds
milling, teeming
not so much confused
but absent

The sidewalk procession
ambles slowly
vacant eyes
without soul
or direction
I am awake
hackles raised, aware
among the sleeping
perhaps the dead

The Mountain

L'enfer c'est les autres

Sartre
that poor, tortured soul
is wrong
Hell, and conversely
heaven
are within

---

20 years

Applications, signatures
witnesses
half a life time
to be quietly
dispassionately dissolved
by ink and administration
such is the way of the law

Aeons

Such is my mien
the structure of my soul
that in times past
I would have been
my liege-lord's unwavering shield
the errant knight questing
the pious hammer of the church
or as heretic scourged

Monday

I was awoken
the downpour fading
as suddenly as it came

Thoughts turn again
to solitude
the hollow pursuit of money

Days spent measured
by hours spent for profit
margins and utilization

Nights searched in silence
paths that I must seek
learn to walk alone

Unbalanced

This sword
leans forward
it's spirit impatient
seeks the cut
to leap forth
from my hand

Mirror

Before me
I see
an alien arraigned
in human flesh
unspoken man, ignorant
that he is god
Roland and the oliphant
the spirit-sword bright
a path
beyond the stars

Sunder

I stand at
the crossroads
alone now
my paths await
their choosing

Call

Like Tuor, before me
stirred in unquiet
before the waves
messenger of Ulmo
drawn to the deeps
the sea-longing
no peace beneath

beech or elm

Love

To have, to hold
to let go
golden chains I have held
selfishly
released and sundered

I have unlatched the cage
she flies
soars free
seeking her own skies
her destinies
beyond me

Fallen

Painted feathers
adorn flesh
wings on the flightless
there are no angels
here
beneath heaven

Geasa

Laws woven

The Mountain

into the fabric
of my being
to never refuse aid
be they friend
or foe
my shield to succour
those in need

Enter not without invitation
and seek not the same

Grid's rod
And Baldr's mistletoe

Muse

The world falls away
clarity, silence
eternity within
a moment

I am but
a witness

Images, words
swell, the spring
flows over
coursing forth
cannot, will not
be contained

Grace

I picked up
the fallen branch
dust swirled
hung in the air
there
by the grace of the Gods
go I

Cliffs above the bay

I turned the motor off
and sat in silence
looking out over the bay

The waves whisper below
my thoughts turning
my father
the lessons he taught
and did not teach

Clouds sheeting the sun
my eyes searching
horizons between islands
paths among hills
within my own heart

We all remember our first

The Mountain

        I was young
      six, perhaps seven
       the kid, running
       tears streaming
        grabs my arm
      pleading for help
       chased by three

    He wasn't my friend
  always teasing, sneering
     holes in my shoes
     no school uniform
      public housing

Stand aside, said the three
  he's not your problem
     not your friend

     I shook my head
 he had asked for my help
    three should never
     persecute one

     I learnt much
       that day
the taste of blood and dirt
   my knuckles skinned
    battle-joy fierce
     my laughter
as blows rained down
      upon me
the red cloud descending
   for the first time

The Mountain

Bloodied, yet
the absence of pain
as I stood
again and again
the kid got away
unscathed

I did not
neither
did the three

The signs

They whisper
shout
urge
buy, you must buy

Buy what?
A moments gratification
sensation fleeting
a moment
or a month
distractions
from voids within

Alchemy

What is broken

The Mountain

crumbling
falling away
those still standing
from ashes and dust
will tend
to new flowers
build again
bright realms and worlds

Stasis

Eat, sleep
repeat
clocks spin
sun winds
time without meaning
I watch
as this body moves
it is not me
not mine
neurons fire, senses
within and without
neutered
by the void

Perth

Here
in this city
I can see

the sky

Gate

The latch falls
into place
the sound
drowned
by silence

Hourglass

The tighter the grip
the faster the sand flows
falling through fingers
taken by the wind

Firmament

I remember
as a child
on the edge of the surf
hot sun over
cool water around
swirling

I remember
the wave surge
sweeping me from my feet

The Mountain

tumbled by the foam

I remember
all that it took
to stop the wild waters
from carrying me
where they may
was for me
to just
stand up

Migraines, deserts

Through sand
my ankles drag
gritty sight, white glare
synapses grind

The test

I thought myself strong
gifted with ability
to lift and carry
heavy, far and long

Of true strength
that is only one kind
or a fraction thereof
Injured, no longer able
to lift and carry

The Mountain

I found myself
bereft of strength
as I knew it
weak

Now, like Samson
shorn and sightless
amongst the pillars
strength of sinew returns
and with it, have I
sight, understanding
knowledge
of what strength truly is

Stockholm

I could lie here
amongst the summer flowers
shaded by spruce and hill
the sun slipping
beyond the waters

I could lie here
forgetting, forgotten
into the earth
unto the skies

40th

The Mountain

It's not worth the time
to sit, think of clever words
yet still I'm writing

Sickness

Noon
and I fade
my tide drawing out
a couple of pills
some water

I roll up my sleeves
the day's work
is not yet done

June

Sliver moon, silver
on darkening horizon
distant, yet within

Training

Water streams from above
without warning
sky cool, clear
halls filled with light

Nemo iudex in causa sua

Sunlight streams in empty space
a corner turned, voices fade
open scars, a quiet place
scales on which the heart is weighed

No harvest

I've stared at this page
too long
this field unploughed
let alone harrowed
no seed have I to sow
and still
the page lies bare

Team function

I knew it was a mistake to come
yet I came anyway
a sense of obligation
expectation
of the normal
the right thing to do

So I came and stood
at the edge of it all
drink in hand
awkward, alone

The Mountain

I knew it was a mistake to come
I cannot explain why
the panic, hackles raised
by noise, lights, faces
conversation
I cannot explain
what you do not understand

I knew it was a mistake to come

My drink now drunk
I slip outside, away
into the cold night air
the overload escaped
but not the sense of shame

Pebble

As the ripples calm
all can be seen
what lies within the circle
and without
the lilies and the reeds
the waters and the shore

Forge

Read the words
I have written

The Mountain

then burn them
from your mind
and do the same
with me

Clouded Skies

Limits placed
by perception
not reality

Better left unsaid

I spoke
with immediate regret
words once released
never recalled
the resulting silence
said everything

Do I understand? no
but that doesn't matter
a long list
of things, people
beyond my ken

---

33 1/3

Swords bare

The Mountain

      between us
      either I die
      you die
      or both

Prosopagnosia

I see them looking
glances from the other table
faces, eyes
alive and moving
yet to me
blank, opaque

I look away
nothing to see here
nothing to see there

Fading of the day

Paper scraps litter
unfinished lines
sentences half said
messages incomplete
not that I would
have the right words
not that you would
read them, reply

Hero

There are no heroes
the women and men
those who are
scholars, monarchs
warriors and priests
gods in human form
are gone
the stuff of myth
legends of aeons past
their peerage not seen
amongst us

We are fallen
degenerate in form
spirit and mind
so far removed
from truth
that nobility
honour
true humanity
impossible
never to be
achieved

Tuath Dé

I see my reflection
for a moment
through the glamour

I cast my shadow
it betrays
my hidden form
I walk the shores
of the world of men
trespassing unseen

Cuchulainn

A raven descends
heralds the death
of the light

Fallen, unfallen
the Gáe Bolg
flowers no more

Beneath Yggdrasil's boughs

I stand
here
on the shoulders
of giants
in the company
of gods
within a fellowship
of heroes

Women and men
of renown

The Mountain

courage
clear sighted

Demons
of doubt
whisper
I do not belong
yet here
I stand

Obituary

I dreamt
that I died

Yet I die
countless deaths
every second

My death
(as if it is 'mine')
means little
nothing
to me
less
to you

In death
life
and life
death

The Mountain

there is
nothing
else

Water's edge

The space between
water
earth, sky
a surface
perfectly defined
distinct
but does not
exist

High tide, low

The tide creeps in
quiet, dark
lapping
at my feet
It whispers
to no one
but me
mocks
scorns

Breathe
see it
for what it is

The Mountain

ephemeral

This, too
shall pass

Black, and white

I blame myself
often
if not always

Not you
I don't understand
you
I barely understand
Me

You, I cannot fathom
I cannot fault
what I don't
understand
so then
I just blame me

---

25 April

This day, every year
acutely aware
of my chest
unburdened

The Mountain

by ornaments
awards
of service

I served
yet did I serve enough
no blood shed I
nor tears

I am unworthy
of those
around me
who do
who have
and of the spirits
of those gone before

Lest we forget

Icarus

O Sun
I flew too close
and fell
no longer
can I behold you
your gaze
turned away

Yet
for a moment

The Mountain

a lifetime
we were
one

Working late

I sit
blank, empty
as the page in front of me
The office
falls silent
the voices fade away

I sit
quiet, empty
as the corridors around me

Shadow

Was I ever really
here, there
no substance, or form
could I be seen
or was it that
your eye
saw
what I truly was
the absence
of anything at all

Flood

Silently, and swift
rose the waters
caring nought
for life, or death
like the wild and ancient Gods
that called them forth

Inconsequential
and unnoticed
the triumphs and dross
of man
swept away

Literary contortionism

I, too, could write a poem
with words twisting, spiraling
more complex than they need to be
for the sake of the 'art'
But, then, I read yours
doing just that
and my eyes glaze over

So, then, I will write a poem
with words that say
exactly what they mean
no more, and no less

Effort

All my errors
mistakes
the harm
I have caused
have been when
I doubted, feared
tried to be
who, what
I am not

Eight directions

To go
nowhere
is not
as easy
as it seems

Circles

I find purpose
meaning
in death
and thus
I find
Life

Elysia

All of us walk
the Elysian fields
a few of us bathe
in radiant skies
and gardens fragrant
most of us feel
the thorns

Winter skies in Autumn

I sat down to write
to you
yet I cannot explain
when you haven't said why
and I lack the courage
to ask

By these signs

The clear, cold dawn of my sight
twisted iron at my throat
the bond of my word
silvered steel at my hand
the ocean of my will

Forgive

All this time
I sought
your forgiveness
and I
only ever
needed
my own

Next
Go upstream
find the source
what then?

Climb the mountain

Camden Haven

Wood fire smoke
hearkens childhood days
solitude and bliss
among redgum shaded hills
clear, cold streams
sun-curtained glades
where the chattering mind
falls silent

Change

It is not
whether
the boat
can withstand
the storm

It is
simply
if you have
skill, to steer
strength, to stand fast
courage, to face
the rising waves
the height of their peaks
the depth of their troughs

Half

If God is good
and evil, the devil
then both are
incomplete

Trample them down
on the path
and go
beyond

Question

Questions that go
unanswered
silence is
the riposte

No more shall
or needs
be said
at all

Mirrors

The mirrors
reveal
almost as much
as they hide

Anodyne seas

I would rather fall
torn by fire and metal
than to live
this unlife
torpor
drowning
in these anodyne seas

Oil and water

I immerse myself in the world
walk amongst those
who look like me
but that I am not like

I plunge in, dive
no matter how deep
or how long
I remain insolute
myself, and apart

I look through the window
at the world
there is no door to find

I am content
the world is not mine
nor I the world's

Tree fall

Words written
spoken out loud
no ears to listen

Words written
hidden
not given voice

Moment(um)

What is there to wait for
a moment
this moment
eternity within
a single breath

There is nothing else
but to act
without thought
doubt, or fear

In acting
victory
over the self

The first stone

The sins
errors
of all mankind
have I made
I can see
Within

I can cast
no stone

The night before

Two blankets
one bed
together
yet separate

All, and nothing

I see in all directions
horizons
out-with
and within
my gaze
pierces
minds
and heavens

Yet
I cannot see
what is hidden
before me
in plain view

Fool

For which am I
the greater fool -
in telling myself
such blatant lies

The Mountain

or for then
believing?

Facebook

Logging in
scrolling
it does little more
than highlight
a world
society
culture
that I do not
know, understand
where I cannot
will not
belong

Knowing, unknowing

When I say
that I do not know
the answer is
the sum
of its parts

Unnamed

The highest

The Mountain

>
>   greatest
>   most perfect
>   poetry
>   has no pen, paper
>   words
>
>   Poetry
>   true poetry
>   was lost
>   when man
>   forgot
>   that he was
>   himself
>   a god

Vanity Fair

>   There is naught here
>   of worth
>   neither bauble, beast
>   or man
>
>   Go amongst, pilgrim
>   the hue and cry
>   the pressing flesh
>   go amongst
>   yet apart
>   and through

Annus

New Year's Eve
simmers, sears
as if to burn away
all trace
of the year gone

In the end
it's another day
another year
the same as
those gone
and yet to come

Birdsong

Sharp and clear
the birdsong
across concrete hills

Red cloud

Insensate
sight, sound, pain falls away
the red cloud rises

No iron or fire can bite
my shield, I gnaw
the red cloud descends

The Mountain

The gods are within
of the bear, wolf, boar
the red cloud burns

Crowd, silence

Already hidden
shadow, within shadow
their faces
hidden further still

Remains of the hours

Absence
drowns out presence

Silence
subdues all clamour

Time
passes yet
remains

Sun, and air

The grass rides the winds
sways, bends, breathes

The Mountain

without care or fear
neither tense, nor relaxed
it simply, and only
is

Leaf

The leaf falls
whether in its time
blown by autumn winds
or plucked by wanton hand
it matters little

The leaf falls
settles
fades
returns
to earth, and tree

Through gates

I hear the wind
taste its salt
it speaks of
winter's cold
stone grey waves
on horizons

Walls

I build these walls
carefully
stone by unhewn stone

I shape these walls
quietly
in silence, unseen

These walls
hide me from you
protect me from the world
and the world
from me
shade me from
the sun, moon, stars
and the eyes of men

I build these walls
swiftly
ere the light of day

Chrysalis

This ill-fitting flesh
chafes and strangles
a chrysalis of sinew and nerve
I feel it erode, decay

The Mountain

with it an urgency, growing

I must find the way
to escape, break loose
lest with it, I die
and be cast into
oblivion

The surface and the water deep

I'm not quick
the currents of my mind
run slower
deeper than most

The cast stone leaves
surface unrippled
sinks beneath
and is weighed
measured, considered
processed
and eventually
be it minutes, weeks, years
understood

The currents
deep, slow
move
the surface
unrippled still

The Mountain

One

I'm tired

Long way from home
a home
I do not know
and have never seen

Lost in a land, a world
amongst peoples strange
customs peculiar
language without translation

An outsider
alien
apart
I am not one of you
that much I know
my plane is other
and I do not belong
in yours

What then, am I
A god clothed in mortal flesh
Angel, fallen and bound
A devil, unknowing
or just mad, deluded
insane

It matters not
I'm weary
and I wait

The Mountain

to be summoned
home

Anatomy

This flesh, clothing
is not a part of me
yet I am bound within
enmeshed and imprisoned

Binary

All or nothing
in all things
nothing in between
people
action
behaviour
coded
feeling
thinking

Alpha or omega
zenith or nadir
black or white
heaven or hell
0 or 1

What remains

What remains unsaid
the iceberg mass
beneath the waters
forever unseen, unheard
things I would say to you
but never will

That which is said, remains
above the waves
for better or ill
or nothing at all

Absolute

If absolute: zero
absence of sound, light
heat
undisturbed, unpolluted
by wave or particle

If absolute: all
bright, clear
the sun
burning, consuming, creating
everything
If absolute: god
alpha and omega
zero and all
what then lies

The Mountain

above, beyond?

Overreach

Water will return to its level
tides withdraw
neither too high, nor too low
balance and the centre
I stretch, strain
try to be
what I am not
thus
I am not
being me

Centre, and the balance
waking, and the dream
withdraw, not into myself
but back to who I am

Waking

A half-smile
turned
and was gone
I had foreseen the blade
but not
how sharp the cut
nor how deep
the wound

Poetry?

It's a rare thing
exceedingly so
words, stanzas
soaring, beauty
poetry

Instead we find
random, meaningless
incoherent
sewage

The ramblings of the mad
the hurt, confused
painfully written and more
painfully read

A few words

I cannot write a poem
not true poetry
the subtle, unseen
deep magic
of which we are currents
in the endless seas

Of what can be written
where words cannot

The Mountain

be spoken
where words do not exist
of words held back
unspoken
the things I cannot say

Wasted effort

Spin in circles
centrifugal
drawing in, casting out
never still, yet never
moving

Unknowing

I don't know myself
yet
I do know what I
have done, chosen
and allowed myself to be

Mirror

My reflection betrays me
unwilling to meet my own eye
loath of what I see
Am I what I behold?

The Mountain

Broken, flawed
monstrous

God made man
in his own image
yet Nephilim, am I

Leaves

Not quite invisible
as unseen, I sit
the world turns
skies remain
people, on foot or wheel
hurry here, there
never still
leaves in the wind

Madding crowd

Belonging comes
from knowing the self
and what's around
are one, and same

I do not belong
out there
I belong
in here

The Mountain

Causa mortis

The blood is let
and the fire contained
the light, approaching
is both tunnel's end
and the beginning of the sky

Fever

The fever has broken
that headstrong wave
of delirium, mania
dissipates, recedes

Left behind are
clear, introspective pools
still and quiet skies
trees seeking the sun

Waves may peak
and trough, yet
the true nature of things
remains as it ever was
unchanged

Useful Idiot

Little more than an ox
carries loads

The Mountain

moves from here to there
keeps hands from being soiled
by dirt, or blood

Naivety... trusting all
believing every word
to be sacrificed, pawned
without a second thought

Such is his worth

Ephemeral

It will pass
the wave troughs, peaks
runs to endless shores

It will pass
gales whip, dancing
singing to the skies

It will pass
daylight giving to dark
circling to the sun

The bay of every

The waters deep, cold
I, a swimmer uncertain
and yet all too brash

The Mountain

I plunge again, again
currents shallow and deep
sweep away or dash
against rock and reef

The sea unforgiving
it's mastery, perhaps, beyond me
I plunge again, again

The sound of

The written word, unread
the spoken then unheard
it matters little, or not at all
an exhalation of breath
serves its own purpose

Frame

Words that I speak
and questions in frame
to me, clear, each word speaking
precisely its meaning, no less
and no more

Yet I see the glances
furrowed brows
I hear the questions
responses, answers

The Mountain

misinterpreted meanings
unrelated to the query

It is me, in truth
but also, it is you
I speak not your language
you fail to understand mine

I tire of explaining, silence
will I thus embrace

Perception

Arrogance, or an air of superiority
no difference, perhaps
indifference
I cannot be other
than myself

Peregrinus mens

Hail, foreigner
you look like us
yet your customs betray you
and your words peculiar

I can see in your eyes
you cannot comprehend
the simplest of things, nuances
speech, without speaking

The Mountain

and the words between words

You share our skin, our blood
yet you walk among us
both here, and there
between this world, and another

From whence you came
and to where?

You cannot say, nor
can I understand

City office

White noise drone of traffic below
fingers on keyboard staccato
muted voices in business drone
a single magpie warbles

Thoughts

She asked what I was thinking
I did not know how to answer

Thoughts there were, and many
like leaves, and flowers
borne away on the stream
as I just watched them go by

The Mountain

Sol

The few awakened
unbound by Tellurian slumber
witness the eastern ascent
of God, radiant
shadows flee, fade
and we are reborn

Going home

You'll be back, they say
and we laugh
they know, as I do
the anodyne sea
the house of sleep
that awaits me

My sword sheathed, discarded
I will strain
against Lethean bonds
in cells of suburbia
rusting, my arms
they whisper in truth
that I should be doing, living
should be
something more than this

In quiet places

The Mountain

The cool, dark earth
below, above
trees breathe
here, the gods
in silent halls dwell

Et tu?

The foe beneath the walls
may clamour and cry
their hatred in hideous din
yet, beware the danger
of the smile
words hushed in corners
the slender knife
a loosing of the gates
from within

Simplicity

The simplest lessons
are the most often forgotten:
eat when hungry
when tired, sleep
drink to slake thirst
and always
breathe

Obol

The river wide
clear and cool
where the road ends
then begins

Unwritten

I thought myself
clever, perhaps wise
yet the empty page
the fallow pen
I cannot overcome

Sun-warmed shoulders and countless skies

To the hills, the heights above
or down streams to the endless sea
the paths unchosen, untrod
are forever calling to me

Leaves in the wind

I want to talk to you
yet the words
do not so much escape
as they are

The Mountain

uncaught, and unfound
thus, I sit
in silence
and listen

Shadows fall

Whispering unseen
in quiet places
devils sow
loneliness, and doubt

Zero sum

Death comes soon enough
I seek not to hasten it
neither to prolong

And thus, I perceived it

Gnawing, the fears:
sins, errors and flaws
are bared for all to see
undeserving of what I have
of anything
it would seem only right, and just
for it all to be swept away
or rather, for me
to be cast down, aside

The Mountain

>
> never again to sully
> and my name, spoken not
> to lose everything
> of redemption, salvation
> there is none
> only exile and damnation
> my eyes covered over
> to hide me from the scorn in yours
> hidden, the shame in mine

Neither

> Shattering of glass
> the breaking of things creates
> beginning, or end?

Unfallen (RIP Tony Rokov)

> He died as he lived
> unbowed, unmastered, fearless
> his eyes to the sky

Until next time

> The airplane climbs
> into the boundless sky
> what was tomorrow
> now is

Words

The placement of words
just so
makes the curse
or song

Sisyphus

Leaving early but
never on time
when it's all too hard
in gardens lie
fear like blood stains water
lay down your oar
dead-weight - or worse
the drowning one who clings
unwilling to swim
pulls others beneath the water
for a time I chose
to be your Sisyphus
at the foot of the hill
you remain

Under which we march

Thunder rumbles slow
rain falling from leaden skies

The Mountain

such a wondrous thing!

Within

I dreamed that I slept
and in sleep, that I died
all was quiet, still
the troubles and the din
of the tremulous world
froth tossed by wind
on the ocean
deep, unmoved, eternal

Distill

Yesterday, I died
tomorrow, I live again
neither existed

Write a poem

Write a poem, they said
it sure will be fun, they said
they say lots of things

All

The Mountain

A single blossom
lies as it fell, placed just so
says everything

Brick walls

If you cannot break through it
climb over, or tunnel beneath

Or walk along it, trace your hand
across its cool mortar
until you find the way around

Or, sit still and see
each brick for what it is
examine its nature, that which
of what it is made
what binds them together
and then, brick by brick
tear it down

Uncertainty

Words, often misused
said without being meant
spoken without truth
belying true meaning and intention.
the seen mass
of the iceberg of communication

The Mountain

For me, the darkening waters
glass-cold and hard
hide what is beneath
I, as one blind
can only turn my ear
to that which is said
and not what is meant

Turn to home

It can't be helped...
the currents swell and sweep away
sink and drown, or swim

Change

Unexpected winds
confound, confuse and dismay
leaves swirl and dance

Bury

Drive my words like nails
into the earth, hidden
where none can read them, nor hear.
let them there lie
quiet, silent, fading
unknown, therefore unlearned
unable to be forgotten, for they

The Mountain

are beyond memory
this is where they belong
among whispering leaves
the cool, dark earth
and quiet, unseeing things

Rise and fall

Light, colour, song
are tinged, tainted, shadowed, black
the mountain storm-sieged

Highway

Stars frost ink-black skies
above dusty country roads
portrait of silence

War

Waiting
shadows rise and fall
the demons of the mind
test - as is their nature
teach - for those willing
to learn
in the here
and the now
the answer

Shine

The clearest diamond
is nothing but grease and coal
the forge fires burn white

Dam walls

Rocks in the water
or streams flowing through mountains
river runs to sea

Memoria in aeterna

Having passed, forget;
it never was anyway
smoke before the wind

Au courant

As the newborn child
gently slips into life's sleep
dream and the waking

The Mountain

Fire

When the one flame ends
Where does the other begin
embers on the sands

Absolute

In absence of light
and matter, just perfection
still, we fear the dark

Hidden in plain view

Losing all meaning
and gaining everything
sit, and ponder this

Aeon

Sands run through fingers
water runs narrow and swift
Canute and the tide

Form

I see you, but not

The Mountain

who you are, why or the how
particles of light

Importance

The important things
are rarely ever thus so
papers in the wind

Extremes

Flagellation, or
masturbation - either way
here write the poets

Tide

Leaden sky, green waves,
a sand grain on the long shore
I am one, none, all

Tea

Floating on water
the leaves green, brown and fragrant
steam rising in thanks

Waves

Where does the mind lie
tossed among the foam and wind
or below, deep, still

September

Subdued is the heart,
wild and unfettered, the mind
storms and gales on seas

Morning star

The dawn approaches
quietly over the bay
magpie voices soar

Mirage

The mind a mirror
what then is it reflecting
no dust can gather

Storm's end

The rains have stopped now

The Mountain

darkening clouds threaten still
waiting for the sun

Mountain road

Ascending the peak
what is the next step forward
descend, climb again

Enervation

Shadows close, gather
dim on the edges of sight
winter will soon yield

Wolf

Hold now - taste the wind
a subtle shift, scent of change
the new day is born

Five rivers

Place not the obol
on my tongue - I need it not
for me, skies beyond

The bow, the sunlit glade

Forcing the arrow
will break it, or send it wide
with words; doubly so

Steel

The nail that pierces
binds, holds, rusts, kills, enlightens
therein, the riddle

Poet

I am not
a poet

A poet is one who
makes flowers with words
rhythms and rhymes
stands up in front of crowds
and proclaims
here am I, I am
a poet

I am
a mirror
a river
the sky
a man

no more
no less

I am not
a poet

Momentum

Say nothing, listen
Winter greets Summer at the door
perfect, just perfect

Anxiety

When unable to
define between real, unreal
all then becomes true

Atonement

The burden of shame
of past wrong, sin and error
fueling the furnace

Automation

When we have devolved
everything, and ourselves
turn off to switch on

Tools

When a useful thing
has fulfilled its function
cast it then aside

Crossroads

Standing hesitant
paralysed by choices
all roads lead to God

Lost words

I left a poem behind
and with it
the pen that wrote it
paper which it wore.
it wasn't mine, the same
that I cannot claim to own
anything

I cannot recall its words
but it spoke of departures
darkening windows

The Mountain

pre-dawn skies
and the hope of, some day
return

Paths well worn

Conversations circle
glass gathers dust
warm streams of sunlight
from the East

Jewel

Evening star burns
cold in my distant eye
a journey of light

Complete

A single gum tree
root to bough, Heaven and Earth
and all things between

Roster's end

The time has come
the time is now

The Mountain

now I must bid adieu
homeward bound
safe and sound
to sleep enough for two

Beloved

Her name, names her so
yet I am here, not there
with the breaking morn
I will return
just to leave again

A narrow path

The sky turns, the Sun bound
westward
and ever on
I shake free
the dust
and follow

Perhaps

The realisation that, perhaps
it's time to go.
the work here is done -
the work is never done -
and i am called to hearth and home.

The Mountain

    turn the wheel down
    a new, different road
    look not behind
    lest I remain
    when new horizons call
    a quiet withdrawal
    a few warm farewells
    the closing and opening
    of doors

Locus

Fickle is the mind
fallen leaf blown, turning in
Autumn's playful winds

Eating lunch

Simple things, and pure
water, air, the laughter of a child
a warm winter Sun

Carvings in timber,
hewn by a forgotten, forgetting hand
and yet still remains.

Each moment a tale
a sudden fragrance, a sound
the illusion of time.

The Mountain

Eat rice, drink water,
breathe in - and then out again
such wonder, perfection!

A new day

Their smile was gone
and with it
the Sun
today waits
expectant

Artificial

Darkness is merely
the absence of light
grey does not exist

Change

Frogs leap, bright fish flash
stone splashes lotus flowers
all is still again

Why the silence

The well is not dry

the waters lie calm and clear
nothing spills over

Tidings

Becoming aware
of battles you had not seen
trust, carry water

Again

Sunrise rust-blossom
soaks across the horizon
this much do I know

Morning

Unnoticed almost
beneath lurid fluorescence
dawn soars above us

Mania

The grasping at things
to possess, to have and hold
falling through fingers

Sunlight

Sunlight in slivers
streams cool through the tattered clouds
glimpses of the Gods

Sol

Stand beneath the Sun
unbowed before the God-King
thus am I blessed

Quietude

Muted colours, light
solemn skies wrought of shadow
winter's silent heart

Impermanence

Foam-flicker on waves
which know not themselves
but the oceans
and the endless skies

Paradigm

The Mountain

Life is never good
nor is it ever evil
sun goes down, comes up

Pilbara

Tired, ancient land
worn to dust and rusted skies
in endless summer

Illusion, delusion

We see in waters
only reflection, mirage
heaven is not there

The passing of a man (a belated eulogy)

I killed my father
it was easy, really - he was already half-dead
a final nod, the flick of a switch...
holding his hand felt like holding
his head underwater
a kindness, a mercy, a murder
my hand on his brow, his sweat
as he struggled to breathe
feebly, to live and to die
there was no turning back, no other choice - it was over

The Mountain

before it began

I killed my father
a man I barely knew
there was no one else to do it, only me
no one else would come.
i grieved, alone
for him, for myself
for a dad I never had
a grandfather my children knew existed
but had never known or seen
grief, or was it anger
slow-burning

I killed my father
then gathered his meagre belongings
emptied his home, cleaned
what could not be cleaned
a decrepit shoe-box caravan
in a corner of a hopeless ghetto
there was little to be found, nothing
to be saved

I felt shame, heavy and deep
that he had lived - and died - this way
that he had let this come to pass
and that I had done the same

Beyond the fences

As it always does

The Mountain

flattering the perfect sky
mirror-glass waters

Sunday

Black birds in pale sky
ram-head torc upon my throat
silence behind all

Hurt, wrong and anger

I can argue points
or hear what she has to say
winter's mirror clear

Different

Everything changes
this is not a lament, no
everything's the same

Waste

Much has been said here
without meaning, direction
words, power: misspent

The Mountain

Waters

Shallow waters run
swift, noisily chattering
deep currents slow, still

Not forgotten, unknown

The Song was sung
no one heard - it fell only upon
quiet leaves
a prayer, sharp and full
falling into silence
and was gone
it mattered not, yet
while it soared
it was everything

Blood

I can feel life, heat
the torrent of crimson fire
this too falls to dust

Empty vessels

When nothing appears
it's not such a bad thing to have

mindful, or mind full

Perception

What is perceived to be
is then real - reality
truth then subjective

Turning

She came to me then
Looking for solace, a friend
I was there but lost

Withdrawal symptoms

I refuse to talk
of the pains and fevers
only of the Gods

Mercy

Were anyone to ask
For quarter, help - even foes
honour binds me close

Old fashioned

Born centuries late
ideals of things long extinct
chivalry, valour

Breath

Where breath is, is life
awakening is only
breathing in, then out

Brevity

Brevity is but
saying what needs to be said
any more is waste

Moment

There is no ending
ergo - nothing has begun
there is only now

Fight through

Fight through!

the soldier knows
that to stop is to die
battle, and thus, life

Eyes cast down

Darkness, sorrow, pain
the poets are bleeding well
there's light here too, friends

Offering

The tendrils of smoke
turn slow, translucent and black
ghosts, forgotten, fade

Names, labels

Naming a poem is
like naming the air, moon or sun
none of these are mine

Winding

The changes, she sits waiting
in time, the ravens fall
seasons fade to new incarnations

The Mountain

memories imbue them all
the silence, she looks skyward
all moments are but one
the passage of the fallen leaf
where quiet waters run
the cycle, she returns anew
what once, is now again
unending begets unbeginning
yet the hidden paths ascend

Paresthesia

Disjointed, and dismembered
why do the words
always run red
it's no coming down when coming clean
siren's song muted, no longer
grip the anchor to my neck
with the lightning bolts behind the eyes
she sees the clouds in silver linings
the rain in crystal skies
cool brow under fevered hands
undercurrents, under pulling
while the surface, mirror-still
with the lightning bolts behind the eyes
short-circuit, self-short-changing
hibernation from the skies

Blade

I take you with the salt
and everything
you say and do
are knives

Sparks

Sparks flicker behind
the eye, on the edge of sight
as real as nothing

Drain

Water falls cold and clear
from the pipe to the concrete
the world disappears

Dragonflies

Dragonflies dancing
graceful ballet of the air
there is nothing more

Conference

A downward spiral

The Mountain

suggests a destination
endless meeting talk

Wanderer

I wander out there
when I am only inside
only I and the I

I?

In sinew lies misbegotten faith
the straw adrift on oceans cruel
from which no salvation could ever ensue
the rapier wit, the cleverest of tongues
could ever erode truth's stone
arrogance humbled as fires are quenched
gone, with ashes as scars soon scattered
bones crumble to naught, to dust
whether in grave gilded or carrion spoil
what then remains, when remains are none?
what currents slip into the river wide
that which we say is 'I' becomes
'I' no more, that false ego shatters
illusion fades, as mist before the sun
and we return, from whence we came
from whence we never departed

Dream

The Sun draws near to Earth
somewhere; but not here
white shatters, spills into colour
and fades into distance
the heroes came, but they
fell - as do they all
into dust and memory
where truth gives way
to what they want to be told
memories born by the smallest things
whispering grass, a fragrance past
and time stands still
the dreams no more to return
but dreams, within themselves

Haven

Paper-thin and cool breeze
the sun warming tired faces
home away from home

Part

Standing in one place,
yet I am not here or there
fragmented, not whole

www.ingramcontent.com/pod-product-compliance
Lightning Source LLC
Chambersburg PA
CBHW032044290426

44110CB00012B/938